Whole Language Evaluation

Reading, Writing, and Spelling For the Intermediate Grades

By Jill Eggleton

Contents

The sun makes the moon shine.

The sun makes the daylight. The sun shines on the earth.

What makes the light on the moon?

Introduction

Monitoring and evaluation are important parts of teaching and learning.

Monitoring involves the collecting and recording of information in many different ways—both formally and informally—by listening to children read, observing children as they read, collecting samples of work, using appropriate checklists, and discussing with parents.

Evaluation involves analyzing the data gathered and suggesting strategies for improvement.

Evaluation should be used in conjunction with monitoring to let the children know their achievements and find out what they need to know next, thereby helping them to be more responsible for their own learning.

The monitoring and evaluation process also helps teachers to choose the materials and set specific objectives that will help children to be as successful as possible.

Monitoring: The checking or keeping of a continuous record.	**Evaluation: The analysis of the data gathered.**
Monitoring should be:	Evaluation should be:
• ongoing. • an integral part of the class program. • an important part of teaching because a teacher is able to: — Find out where the child is at. — Learn what the child already knows. — Find out what the child needs to know next. — Match learning experiences to individuals or groups. — Select the right materials. — Organize the class program to the best advantage of individual children.	• ongoing, accurate, and objective. • concerned with specifics and not generalities. • based on the results of careful and thoughtful monitoring. • concerned with the child's own analysis of progress (i.e., self-evaluation). • an important part of teaching because a teacher is able to: — gauge the effectiveness of the program in action. — judge the effectiveness of teaching strategies used. — use this information to help plan more effectively.

Whole Language Evaluation : For the Intermediate Grades provides a practical guide for the monitoring and evaluation of reading and writing programs for children in the middle years of instruction.

Overview of Reading Program
Fluency-plus Stage

Teachers' Targets and Methods		Children's Targets	Monitoring
To establish an interesting, balanced, and enjoyable program:	By Shared Reading, Guided Reading, Independent Reading, reading to children, paired reading, home reading, providing a wide variety of reading materials for different purposes.	To be aware of a variety of types of literature (e.g., mysteries, fiction, nonfiction, short stories...). To understand that authors and illustrators have individual voices and styles. To show pleasure and enthusiasm in sharing and discussing books.	Observations.
To continue to foster a love of reading:	By an enthusiastic approach and showing children that you value reading.	To show independence in selecting appropriate reading material.	Running records. (Miscue analysis)
To continue to develop the understanding that reading for meaning is paramount:	By asking questions that will lead to a deepening of children's understanding.	To show understanding of and insight into what has been read. To be able to read for a specific purpose.	
To reinforce the use of reading skills to interpret and understand context:	By encouraging children to use a wide variety of reading skills flexibly and independently and by encouraging them to learn from mistakes.	To be able to use reference material to select information. To be able to select main idea, identify theme, identify authors, identify settings, identify plot, identify purpose, identify sequence.	Reading Checklists.
To continue to extend children's vocabulary:	By listening to stories, discussing new vocabulary, and providing varied firsthand experiences for interaction.	To be able to use an index, a table of contents, a glossary, maps, graphs, tables, and diagrams. To know and use the library effectively.	Individual Conferences. (Teacher/Pupil)
To cater to children's individual needs:	By knowing your students' likes, dislikes, strengths, weaknesses; by discussing stories individually read; by taking running records.	To use appropriate cues to identify unknown words and to recheck meanings.	
To encourage independence:	By allowing children to make their own choices of reading material, fostering library independence, and allocating time to Independent Reading.	To be able to predict words and story lines from context.	Self-evaluation.

Reading

Overview of the Reading Program

The overview consists of four parts:

• The teachers' targets—the aims, or objectives.

• The methods—the program used to reach the teachers' targets.

• The children's targets—what the child should achieve at the fluency-plus level.

• Monitoring—the collection of data in a variety of ways.

This overview is at the fluency-plus level. Fluency-plus indicates that the child is an independent, confident, and competent reader. However, all children in the class may not be at the fluency-plus level. They could be at emergent, early, or fluency levels. The overviews for these levels are included in *Whole Language Evaluation* (from the Sunshine Series) by Jill Eggleton.

Note: It must be emphasized that it is not the age of the child that determines where the individual reading program begins, but where the child is at.

Teachers' Targets

To establish an interesting, balanced, and enjoyable program.

To continue to foster a love of reading.

To continue to develop the understanding that reading for meaning is paramount.

To reinforce the use of reading skills to interpret and understand context.

To continue to extend children's vocabulary.

To cater to children's individual needs.

To encourage independence.

Methods for Achieving the Targets

1. **Reading to Children**
2. **Shared Reading**
3. **Guided Reading**
4. **Independent Reading**
5. **Paired Reading**
6. **Home Reading**

1.   Reading to Children

Reading to children should continue to form an important daily part of the class reading program. This is a time for the teacher and children to enjoy stories and expand their reading interests.

2.   Shared Reading

(Ref: *Moving On in Whole Language* by Brian Cutting from the Sunshine Series.)

The purpose of Shared Reading at the fluency-plus level is to delight in and to learn about different genres, different book formats, and different styles and literary qualities and to explore more sophisticated reading skills. By using multiple copies of the shared book (or Big Book), children can be helped to extend their understanding of the materials and reading processes through discussion with peers and the teacher.

During a Shared Reading session, the whole story or just part of the story could be shared, depending on the time allowed and the purpose of reading. The same story could be used over a period of a few days with a new purpose for the re-reading being established each day.   For example, these purposes could include:

— Extending vocabulary.
— Extending understanding of punctuation forms.
— Developing study skills.
— Identifying themes and authors' purposes.
— Identifying settings and plot sequences.

It must be emphasized, however, that there is no set recipe or formula for a Shared Reading session. The teaching of skills occurs as a natural part of the reading process.

Note: If you have a special focus poem for the week, the same procedure can be used as for a shared book. Each child can have a poetry anthology in which the focus poem can be put at the end of the week.

3. Guided Reading

(Ref: *Moving On in Whole Language* by Brian Cutting from the Sunshine Series.)

Guided (Silent) Reading at fluency-plus level is reading for a purpose and discussing what has been discovered. It is "guided" because there is a continuing interaction between children and teacher as they examine their responses to the text.

The following organization could form the basis of the Guided (Silent) Reading program.

• Preparation
Group children according to needs or interests. (Groups should be flexible and change according to individual and teacher needs.)

Select suitable material and identify the reading and writing skills that could be examined naturally within the context of a story. For example:

— Extend vocabulary.
— Practice questioning skills.
— Understand new concepts.
— Develop study skills.

• Reading time
Ask the children to read the story silently.

• Discussion
Following the reading time, teachers and children should come together to:

— Share their findings.
— Share different points of view and support these views by referring to the appropriate text.
— Clarify or extend their understanding by re-reading parts of the text.
— Ask questions concerning difficult vocabulary or meanings of words or phrases.

4. Independent Reading

(Ref: *Moving On in Whole Language* by Brian Cutting from the Sunshine Series.)

In Independent Reading, children choose their own material and read independently at their own pace.

The following suggestions could form the basis for the Independent Reading program.

• Organize a copy of the booklet "My Reading Record" for each child.

- Organize the reading materials that the children will select from. These materials should:

  — Cover a wide variety. (For example: fiction, nonfiction, fables, biographies...)
  — Vary in format. (For example, books—including chapter books and picture books—magazines, newspapers, and reference material, including encyclopedias, an atlas, a thesaurus, and brochures).
  — Be at different levels of difficulty.
  — Be constantly added to with new material.

- Motivate children to read by:

  — Discussing a variety of reading material.
  — Reading to children daily.

- Give children time to initially browse through the range of material that is available. The children can record what they would like to read in the "My Reading Record" booklet.

- Establish the routines for the Independent Reading program, outlining:

  — Daily time for reading.
  — Care of materials.
  — Borrowing and returning organization.
  — The conference time—and what it involves. (See page 24)
  — The sharing and display timetable.
  — Time to browse.

- Establish the routines for children to follow once they have completed their reading.

  Children can:

  — Fill in the "My Reading Record" booklet.
  — Choose an activity to follow the reading.

  For example, children could choose to:

  — Continue to read.
  — Read a favorite part of the book to a group, friend, or class.
  — Share a "message" from a character in the book.
  — Prepare a newspaper advertisement or radio advertisement to sell the book to others.
  — Mime, dramatize, or role play an interesting part.
  — Present some related art or craft activity.
  — Make a list of other books by the same author or list similar themes, plots, characters, etc.
  — Write a letter to the author, giving feedback about the book or asking for more information.

— Write an alternative ending for the book.
— Retell the story in a different way. For example, read and record it onto a tape, using silhouettes.
— Write a family tree of characters from a book.
— Write a cinquain poem about the book.
— List facts you know after reading the book.
— Research the author's background and write a small life history of the author.

5. Paired Reading

Paired Reading is when children choose a partner to read to. The reading material is self-selected. It could be read to a teacher, a peer, a younger or older child, a parent, or some other adult.

6. Home Reading

Children take home self-selected reading material to share with their parents.

A newsletter (see page 33) to parents explaining the purpose of the reading program and suggestions as to how parents can help in the fostering of positive attitudes toward reading is valuable.

Providing Materials to Support the Methods

Teachers in whole-language classrooms provide a variety of reading materials for different purposes. The following suggestions can form the basis of classroom organization of materials.

• Reading-related Learning Centers

Reading-related learning centers can be established in the classroom to help stimulate the children's use of a variety of reading materials. Establish, for example:

<u>A classroom library center</u>
Books for independent reading could be stored here in sections of nonfiction, fairy tales, myths and legends, picture books, chapter books...

Build on the children's already acquired knowledge of the library to foster an independence and enjoyment of reading. The children should know the organizational arrangement of books in the library and how the books and materials are issued.

(Note: Library procedures and skills should not be taught as isolated skills but as a natural part of meeting the needs of the children as they *use* the library.)

A poetry center
Incorporate a variety of poems on cardboard, poetry books, and materials for copying favorite poems or for learning or making anthologies and for writing new poems.

A dictionary center
Incorporate a variety of dictionaries, crosswords, thesauruses, and word games.

An author's center
Incorporate a variety of books on a particular author (including the published books of children in the class).

A magazine center
Incorporate a variety of magazines, comics, and newspapers.

A science center
Incorporate a display of science books on a current theme.

Listening Post center
Incorporate a variety of taped stories (including stories produced by children in the class).

An arts and crafts center
Incorporate books and charts giving instructions on "How to Make…" subjects.

A reference center
Incorporate a variety of reference material, such as encyclopedias, an atlas, a globe, and maps.

The Sunshine books provide both the base for the reading program and the springboard for further reading in literature. All of the Sunshine books, both fiction and nonfiction, can be used for all of the suggested methods—from Reading to to Independent Reading.

Sunshine Books for Use at the Fluency-plus Level

Fiction:

The Trouble with Heathrow
Baby's Breakfast
Seasons
Lost and Found
The Garden Party
Feeling Funny
Anak the Brave
The Wonderhair Hair Restorer
A Pet to the Vet
The New House Villain
Leap Year
Princess Harimau and the Tiger
Tai Taylor is Born
Trouble on the Bus
The Little Round Husband
The New Boy
Tai Taylor and the "Sweet Annie"
Tai Taylor Goes to School
The Best Diver in the World
Iris La Bonga and the Boomerzoomer
The Mad Puppet
The Haunting of Miss Cardamon
Papil
The Stranger from the Sea

The Pop Group
The Man Who Enjoyed Grumbling
The Man Who Never Told the Truth
Crocodile! Crocodile!
The Tree Doctor
Muppy's Ball
A Lion Song
The Little Kite
The King's Treasure
The Funny, Funny Clown Face
The Haunted House
The Big Fish
The Terrible Topsy-Turvy, Tissy-Tossy Tangle
Mr. Rumfitt
Agatha's Brew
A Yabby Tale
Tai Taylor and His Education
The King's Jokes
Iris La Bonga and the Locked Door
White Elephants
Iris La Bonga and the Helpful Taxi Driver
The Girl Who Washed in Moonlight
Time Warp
The Beauty Contest

Fact and Fantasy:

Animals and Air
A Rocket Surprise
Rain, Rivers, and Rain Again
Moving Things
The Humpback Whale
Knights in Armor
The Sea Otter
Chicken Dinner

The Number Cruncher
Wonders of the World
You Are Special
Joy Cowley Writes
The Emperor Penguin
No Place Like Home
The Solar System
The Super Body Fun Fair

Children's Targets

The following Targets Chart outlines the kinds of abilities and skills the children should be aiming to develop and acquire at the fluency-plus level. They are targets that should be encouraged, taught, or reinforced through the variety of reading approaches mentioned in the overview.

CHILDREN'S TARGETS
•   To be aware of a variety of types of literature (e.g., mysteries, fiction, nonfiction, short stories).
•   To understand that authors and illustrators have individual voices and styles.
•   To show pleasure and enthusiasm in sharing and discussing books.
•   To show independence in selecting appropriate reading material.
•   To show understanding of and insight into what has been read.
•   To be able to read for a specific purpose.
•   To be able to use reference material to select information.
•   To be able to select the main idea, identify theme, identify authors, identify settings, identify plot, identify purpose, identify sequence.
•   To be able to use an index, a table of contents, a glossary, maps, graphs, tables, and diagrams.
•   To know and use the library effectively.
•   To use appropriate cues to identify unknown words and to recheck meanings.
•   To be able to predict words and story lines from context.

Monitoring Progress

Monitoring is the process of collecting a variety of information that can be used to find out where children are at and what they need to know next.

To monitor reading at the fluency-plus level, the following methods are used:

1. **Observations**
2. **Running Records**
3. **Self-evaluation**
4. **Reading Checklists**
5. **Individual Conferences**

1. **Observations**

   Observing children carefully and systematically enables teachers to go beyond guesswork or assumption. Observations of a child's reading behavior over a period of time are essential to evaluation.

   At the beginning of the school year, initial observations should be made. The focus of these observations should be to establish the attitude and interest of the child. For example:

   • Does the child read willingly with obvious enjoyment?

   • Does the child become involved in what he or she is reading?

   • Does the child offer to talk about books and participate in book sharing activities?

   • Does the child take books home?

   • Does the child select a variety of material?

   Specific notes on these initial observations should be kept in the "observation" space of the child's "Individual Reading Profile." (See page 26)

   (Note: If a lack of interest is observed, intervention by the teacher would be necessary. Discussion with parents to compare their observations of the child's reading behavior at home would be valuable.)

   Other observations are ongoing throughout the year and should give the teacher an intimate understanding of the child's strengths, needs, and progress.

   These observations would be gained from:

   — Running records.
   — Conferencing in the Independent Reading Program.
   — Self-evaluations.

Observational notes would be made in the appropriate space in the "Individual Reading Profile."

Another suggestion is to initially record observations on a "calendar-like" page:

Observational notes			
Sam: Selecting only nonfiction material.	Tony: Not keen to share — always chooses to continue reading.	Sally: Spends too long on follow-up activity. Needs to read more.	David: Very quick reader. Check understanding.
Hollie: Takes time to select material. Prefers short stories and magazines.	Jarrod: Reads widely. Shows very good understanding of material read.	Rick: Slow to settle to reading. Easily distracted from task.	Jasmine: Always very keen to share materials read. Needs to vary material.

These observations can then be transferred to the child's "Individual Reading Profile" when convenient.

(Note: It is necessary to record only information that is important in making educational decisions when working with parents and pupils. This makes the task manageable.)

2. Running Records

(Ref: Marie Clay—*The Early Detection of Reading Difficulties.*)

Running records describe accurately what actually occurs in the course of reading. Teachers can use them to reflect on and evaluate the reading process through analyzing the child's oral reading miscues.

Running records should be taken at the beginning of each year to get to know the pupils (and to establish reading material that is suitable to their needs) and on a regular basis throughout the year. This can be done by:

• Taking a running record from one of the reading examples included. (See pages 77-101)

• Analyzing this information.

• Making decisions from the analysis of this information about the reading program for each individual.

It is important to take running records on both fiction and nonfiction.

Note: In analyzing errors, consider what the error rate would be if unimportant errors are disregarded. Errors that do not alter meaning at all may be the kind of errors that proficient readers make. Working out the error rate including these errors may give a distorted view of the child's competence.

The purpose of closely observing and analyzing a child's reading behavior in this way is to:
    — Provide teaching points for one-to-one conferencing with the child.
    — To establish Guided Reading groups that will ensure the child is being challenged.
    — To ascertain the child's independent reading level.

The following procedure can be used to observe a child's reading behavior.

a)   Select a reading passage. (See examples on pages 72-101)

b)   Briefly discuss the title.

c)   Get the child to read the passage silently.

d)   Get the child to retell the main points in the passage.

e)   Comment on understanding in the appropriate place on the summary sheet. (See examples, pages 18 and 20.)

f)   Get the child to read the story orally, recording all reading behavior on the running record observation sheet.

g)   Ask one or two questions to further probe the child's understanding of the text.

h)   Analyze the data and fill in the running record summary sheet. (See example, page 18.)

i)   File the information in the "Individual Reading Profile." (See page 50.)

Running Record

The following is a sample running record and completed summary sheet (based on *The Stranger from the Sea* by Lois Burleigh [Sunshine, Level 11].)

Note: The summary sheet would be filed in the child's "Individual Reading Profile."

Summary Sheet — Running Record

Name ..... *Ellen* .... Date .... 14-6 ....

Title ... *The Stranger from the Sea* .... Level $9\frac{1}{2}$ to $10\frac{1}{2}$ year old

Understanding: (Comment on the child's retelling and grasp of main ideas.)

Able to recall some details of story but needed questioning in order to prove a greater understanding.

Observations of reading behavior

- ☐ Self-corrects.
- ☐ Cross-checks one cue source with another.
- ☑ Reads on.
- ☐ Seeks help.
- ☐ Waits.

Analysis of errors

Uses:	Seldom	Sometimes	Usually
Visual cues	☐	☐	☑
Structure cues	☐	☑	☐
Meaning cues	☑	☐	☐

Needs further help to use:

Visual cues ☐

Structure cues ☐

Meaning cues ☐

Reading level
Percentage accuracy = 99 % S.C. Rate 1 : 2

Conclusions:
The above text is Ellen's instructional reading level.

Areas of weakness noted: *Lack of expression*
Using visual cues but not cross-checking with meaning.

Encourage Ellen to read a wide variety of material at her independent reading level to practice fluency. During instructional reading, reinforce the importance of cross-checking cues. Encourage Ellen to retell stories in more detail.

READING

Name: Age: Date:

The Stranger from the Sea
9-1/2 — 10-1/2

On the south coast of the island, Thomas lived alone. He loved to
breathe the fresh salt air and to hear the gentle rhythm of the waves
lapping the shore or breaking on the rocks.

Sometimes he thought he would like to share his life with a wife,
a wife who would want to live in his cottage, smelling the salt air and
listening to the waves. But then Thomas would sigh and put the
matter out of his mind.

Night after night, Thomas sat alone in his cottage, listening to the
waves. One night the seas raged, the wind howled, and the rain beat
down. Suddenly, above the sound of the waves crashing on the
rocks, Thomas heard a knock at the door. On the doorstep stood a
man, wet and bedraggled.

"Come and help!" cried the man. "There's a fishing boat wrecked
on the rocks along the coast. We'll need warm blankets and hot
drinks."

Thomas made a fresh brew of tea and poured it into a thermos
bottle. He packed some food into a bag, put on his hooded oilskin
coat, picked up a few blankets and his lantern, then ran down the path
to the beach.

For hours, Thomas worked alongside the other men to help the
crew of the sinking boat. He waded out to the rocks to assist survivors
ashore. One of the men carried to shore a figure so cold and fragile it
was having difficulty breathing. Thomas put some warm tea into a
mug and offered it to the frail form. Slowly he realized that this was
not one of the fishermen from the wreck, but a young woman.

Thomas turned to the man who had helped her ashore.

"Let us take her up to my cottage. She needs to be away from
this foul weather."

M = meaning = Does it make sense?
S = structure = Does it sound right?
V = visual = Does it look similar?

Analysis

E	SC	E M S V	SC M S
1		m s (v)	
	1		
1	1	m (s)(v)	m s (v)

Write MSV in the
appropriate column and
circle the type of cue the
child has used.

The following is a sample running record and completed summary sheet (based on *Agatha's Brew* by Jack Gabolinscy [Sunshine, Level 9].)

Note: The summary sheet would be filed in the child's "Individual Reading Profile."

Summary Sheet — Running Record

Name ...*Phyllis*.. Date ...*10-6*.......................

Title ...*Agatha's Brew*.. Level ...*8½ to 9½ years old*.....

Understanding: (Comment on the child's retelling and grasp of main ideas.)

Able to recall some details of story but needed questioning in order to prove a greater understanding.

Observations of reading behavior

☑ Self-corrects.

☐ Cross-checks one cue source with another.

☐ Reads on.

☐ Seeks help.

☑ Waits.

Analysis of errors

Uses:	Seldom	Sometimes	Usually
Visual cues	☐	☑	☐
Structure cues	☐	☑	☐
Meaning cues	☐	☑	☐

Needs further help to use:

Visual cues ☑

Structure cues ☑

Meaning cues ☑

Reading level

Percentage accuracy = *96%* S.C. Rate *1 : 3*

Conclusions:
This text is at Phyllis's instructional reading level.

Areas of weakness noted: *Using all cues sometimes but not cross-checking. When confronted with a difficult word tends to wait. Relies on teacher input.*
Not absorbing fully details of the story.

Action to be taken:
Encourage Phyllis to use all cues. Encourage re-running and reading on when coming to an unknown word. Question Phyllis fully about stories read. Endeavor to extend her vocabulary whenever possible.

READING

Name: *Phyllis*   Age: *9·1*   Date:

Agatha's Brew
8-1/2 — 9-1/2

Agatha poured a bottle of tabasco sauce, two tablespoons of cayenne pepper, and half a cup of curry powder into the blender.

"That should make even a jellyfish breathe fire," she said.

Next, she added a cup of salt, a quarter of a bottle of castor oil, the juice of three green lemons, and a cake of soap.

"And that," she said, "should be enough to make any jellyfish spit!"

Lastly, she added a whole bottle of vitamin juice (because it wasn't worth making a magic brew unless it was a strong and energetic one).

Agatha switched on the blender and watched the sharp blades whip the mixture into a frothy, yellowy, reddish-brown porridge. She put her nose over the bowl and sniffed long and deep.

"Wow!" she shrieked.

The hairs on the back of her neck stood up like hedgehog prickles, her ears burned, and her toes curled up in her shoes. "Wow!" she exclaimed. "That's a powerful potion! I'll call it Bazooka Brew."

A fly from the ceiling buzzed down and landed on the blender. It poked its long nose down into the brew and sucked it hungrily.

Agatha watched.

Suddenly the happy buzzing of the/fly changed into a roar like that of a mini-jet at take-off. The fly leaped into the air and zoomed toward the kitchen window.

"Stop!" cried Agatha. But it was too late.

"CRACK!" The fly hit the window at top speed, and a small, round, bullet-like hole appeared in the glass.

"Very strong fly!" said Agatha, watching the fly disappear at supersonic speed. "I might have something here. I better make sure no nasty bees or spiders or bats get any brew."

Analysis

E	SC	E M S V	SC M S
3 1		ⓜⓢv	
	1		m s Ⓥ
1	1	m s Ⓥ	m s Ⓥ
2		m s Ⓥ m s Ⓥ	
1 2		ⓜⓢv	
	1		m s Ⓥ
	1		m s Ⓥ

M = meaning = Does it make sense?
S = structure = Does it sound right?
V = visual = Does it look similar?

Write MSV in the appropriate column, and circle the type of cue the child has used.

21

3.   Self-evaluation

Children should be encouraged to take responsibility for their own learning, to set goals for themselves, and to evaluate their achievements in relation to their goals.

Self-evaluation puts children in charge of their own learning. Children should be encouraged to reflect on their reading behavior and establish what they could change and what they could do to help their reading skills grow. Each reader must discover personally the reading strategies that allow him or her to be a successful reader.

The following are some suggestions to encourage children in self-evaluation.

• Children could fill in the chart on page 14 of the "My Reading Record" booklet.

• Children could fill in their own checklists.

Do I think about what I read?	
Do I read a variety of different material?	
Do I read at home in my spare time?	

• Children could write their own reports to share with their teacher and parents. For example:

Reading report on Things I do well: Things I want to learn: Signed ....

4. Reading Checklists

Reading checklists provide an overview of what the child has achieved. They contain information gained through observations, reading logs, and running records.

Checklists help to remind teachers that evaluation is an ongoing process.

Reading Checklist - Fluency-plus	
Skills: Reads a variety of material—both fiction and nonfiction. Reads for enjoyment and information. Visits and uses the library. Uses reading skills effectively to make sense of text. Is able to skim for information. Selects and integrates relevant information from a range of sources. Selects, organizes, and uses relevant information in self-selected or assigned tasks. **Attitudes:** Shares reading material with others. Contributes to discussion activities. Is keen to extend knowledge and skills.	

Note: If checklists are used, the items being "checked" must be worth evaluating. If there is no sound educational reason for recording information, we need not bother. Checklists can, however, provide a sound organizational structure for gathering information for evaluation purposes.

5. Individual Conferences

The individual conference can be either an informal one or a more formal "appointment-made" conference.

An informal conference is when a teacher observes in "classroom roving" that there is some area of concern and slips alongside a child to discuss and assist.

A formal conference is when an appointment is made between the teacher and pupil.

Conference timetable

Who has a conference today?				
Monday	Tuesday	Wednesday	Thursday	Friday
Sam	Hollie			

Some key elements of the individual conference are the personal interaction, the sharing of enjoyment, and the appreciation of the special features of the story. There is opportunity for the teacher to explore the interests of the reader and to focus on the way reading problems are solved. There are opportunities to monitor reading, diagnose strengths and weaknesses, offer guidance, meet individual needs, and give encouragement.

- Establish the routines for a conference time. The conference could involve:

    — Sharing and discussing interests.
    — Sharing a special feature.
    — Sharing personal experiences.
    — Monitoring reading by taking a running record and diagnosing strengths and weaknesses.
    — Offering guidance to the child by encouraging the selection of appropriate reading materials and discussing the "Individual Reading Profile."
    — Encouraging the child to fill in the chart on page 14 of "My Reading Record."

At the completion of the conference, the "conference sheet" in the child's "Individual Reading Profile" (see page 27) is dated and comments on strengths and weaknesses are entered.

At the conclusion of the conference, the teacher should:

— State things the reader has done well.
— State things particularly enjoyed.
— Ask the child if there are any ways further help can be provided.

Portfolios

Portfolios are a means of storing data and information on a child. The portfolios contain a long-term record of a child's growth and development. These individual portfolios can be cardboard pockets in a filing cabinet or boxes. The portfolios should have the child's name and date of birth.

The "Individual Reading Profile"

The reading information on each child needs to be collated in a way that makes it easily accessible to the teacher and parents.

When the child first enters school, an "Individual File" is established. The data collected over the first year of school (at approximately 5—7 years of age) is accumulated in this file. (Refer to *Whole Language Evaluation* for the primary grades.) After a time, this file will become too bulky, and another method of keeping data needs to be established for children in the intermediate grades. (Note: The original "Individual File" from the primary grades should be kept for reference at a later date, if necessary.)

One suggestion for keeping data at the intermediate-grade level is that each child has two individual profiles: one profile for reading and one for writing and spelling.

In reading, the profile should contain background information that is relevant to reading, the observation notes, the running record summary sheets, the reading checklist, the conference notes, and parent comments.

This "Individual Reading Profile" is used for:

— Giving feedback to the child. (The information in the profile *should* be shared with the child.)
— Sharing with parents during parent interviews.
— Writing written reports for parents.
— Gaining specific information for the cumulative record cards.

At any time during the child's school career, the "Individual Reading Profile" can be used to:

— Show the child what progress has been made over time.
— Illustrate for parents the child's growth.

The "Individual Reading Profile"

The following pages outline the format of the "Individual Reading Profile."

Individual Reading Profile: Page One   Individual Reading Profile: Page Two

Reading Profile	Observations	
Name	**Date**	Teacher Action:
Year .... Grade		
Background information:		
Hobbies and interests		
Likes and dislikes		
Friends		
Sports		
TV and reading		
Ambitions and problems		
Observations (informal)		

Conference Notes
(Record strengths and weaknesses apparent — note action taken.)

Date:

A Sample Running Record and completed summary sheet.

Summary Sheet - Running Record

Name .... Date ....

Title ....Level ....

Understanding (Comment on retelling of story and grasp of main ideas)

| **Observations of Reading behavior.** | **Analysis of Errors** |
| | S/dom S/times Usually |

☐ Self-corrects   Uses visual cues ☐ ☐ ☐
☐ Cross-checks one cue   Structure cues ☐ ☐ ☐
    source with another   Meaning cues ☐ ☐ ☐
☐ Reads on   **Needs further help to use:**
☐ Seeks help   Visual cues ☐
☐ Waits   Structure cues ☐ Meaning cues ☐
Percentage accuracy =   %   S.C rate = 1 :   ☐

Conclusions

Note: Add summary sheet after each running record taken for evaluation purposes

Reading Checklist - Fluency-plus

Skills:

Reads a variety of material (both fiction and nonfiction).

Reads for enjoyment and information.

Visits and uses the library.

Uses strategies effectively to make sense of text.

Is able to skim for information.

Selects and integrates relevant information from a range of sources.

Selects, organizes, and uses relevant information in self-selected or assigned tasks.

Attitudes:

Shares reading material with others.

Contributes to discussion activities.

Is keen to extend knowledge and skills.

Parent comments:

Cumulative Record Cards

A cumulative record is a system of keeping records about each child's individual progress. This cumulative record card provides information that is based on the child's achievements and is transferred from class to class as the child moves. (The cumulative record could also be transferred from school to school when necessary.)

Each child has a cumulative record card. The cumulative record card contains specific information gained from the data gathering. The information (based on fact) is concerned with relevant and important matters and draws attention to the child's current needs and strengths.

Entries should be made on the cumulative record card twice per year. All entries must be signed. Entries will indicate the knowledge a child has, skills attained, and his or her attitude. For example:

*   Does the child read for enjoyment and information according to his or her own interests, needs, and background?

*   Does the child find, select, organize and use information for his or her own purposes?

*   Does the child show an interest in visiting the library and selecting a variety of material?

*   Does the child use reading skills effectively to make sense of the text?

*   Does the child show enthusiasm for reading by the variety of books read?

*   Does the child enjoy contributing to discussions?

A Sample Cumulative Record Card

Name:	Sex:
School:	Date of Birth:
Date first entered school:	

HEALTH FACTORS	WELFARE CONCERNS

Information from previous cumulative record card:

CURRICULUM

LANGUAGE Listening and speaking	Writing
Reading	

Mathematics:

Health:

Science:

Art:

Music:

Social Studies:

Physical Education:

PERSONAL AND SOCIAL DEVELOPMENT

ATTENDANCE	YEAR	TEACHER'S SIGNATURE	DATE

Using the Data

The data collected from observations, self-evaluation, running records, reading checklists, and individual conferences can be used in the following ways:

1. **Evaluating Children's Progress**
   (to give children information about their progress)

2. **Evaluating the Program**
   (to give teachers information about the effectiveness of the program)

3. **Reporting to Parents**

1. Evaluating Children's Progress

Children's progress should be evaluated to give them feedback that will facilitate learning.

The children should understand how their progress is measured and how to use the feedback of the evaluation. Teachers should share the "Individual Reading Profile" with each individual. Using the data gathered in the monitoring process, the teacher should:

• Diagnose the child's difficulties and give a lead as to how he or she might improve.

• Motivate the child to learn further.

• Encourage the child toward self-evaluation.

2. Evaluating the Program

When evaluating the reading program in action, it is important to consider whether or not the teacher's targets are being achieved.

• Is the program balanced? Are a variety of methods and materials being used by both children and teacher?

• Do the children show an enthusiasm for reading?

• Do the children demonstrate a real interest in a variety of reading materials?

• Do the children show an understanding of what they have read?

• Are the children using reading skills effectively to make sense of the text?

- Are the individual needs of each child being catered to? Is the material challenging enough for all children? Are children given enough time to read?

- What still needs to be learned and what new aims and objectives need to be set for the next steps in learning?

As with evaluation of the children's progress, the evaluation of the class program should be based on observation, reflection, analysis, and action.

3. Reporting to Parents

Evaluation should be seen as a partnership between teachers and parents in a joint endeavor to understand and discover the needs of the individual child.

Reports, whether oral or written, should focus upon the learning achievements of the individual child. They should describe the knowledge, skills, and attitudes being developed and should be in sufficient detail for the parents to feel confident that the report informs them about the learning that has occurred.

The following suggestions outline ways that parents and teachers can "keep in touch."

- Outline the reading program in a newsletter. (Give parents the opportunity to participate in, to support, and to respond to the reading program.)

Dear Parents,

The staff of (...........................) welcome you as a parent and look forward to a pleasurable association with you. We would like to share some positive ways you could help your child continue in his/her reading development.

Our purpose is to provide a reading program that is enjoyable and that gives children a wide range of reading experiences. We want children to love reading and to be independent readers.

We will be encouraging children to:

— Read a variety of books.
— Share the stories they have read with others.
— Show an understanding of what they have read.
— Be able to use all aspects of the library correctly.

As parents, you play a vital role in your child's attitude toward reading, and we would be grateful for your continued support.

Your child should be reading for pleasure for a set time each night. Showing an interest in what he or she is reading is most important. You can question your child briefly about the story to ensure that he or she has an understanding of what has been read. Your child might like to share an interesting paragraph or two with you. Sharing a story you might have read that has a similar theme or the same type of book would also be helpful.

Be aware of the reading material your child selects to read. It is important to encourage the reading of a variety of books (e.g., nonfiction, fiction, humor, mysteries). Regular visits to the public library are most valuable.

Draw your child's attention to interesting articles in the newspaper. Get him or her to read these and discuss them with you.

Each week your child will bring home a poetry anthology with a new poem for the week in it. He or she will enjoy sharing this with you and, in return, you may be able to share some poems, as well.

Please do not compare one child with another. They are all individuals and progress at their own rate.

Our aim is to provide a happy, caring environment with each child involved in the learning process.

We would be pleased to discuss any problems or queries that you may have. The education of your child is a partnership.

Yours sincerely,

- After approximately one month of the school year, arrange a parent/teacher discussion. This is a time for the teachers to gain an insight into a child's feelings about school, about likes and dislikes at home and school, topics of conversation, reading and book borrowing habits, about personal ambitions, and about parents' ambitions for their child. Any relevant information is recorded in the "Individual Reading Profile." (See page 28).

- After approximately three months of the school year, an informal interview between teacher and parents is arranged. This is the time for the teacher to formally share with the parents the child's achievements to date and to outline future goals.

The teacher will use data gathered from:

— Observations.
— The "Individual Reading Profile," running records, reading checklists, conference survey, self-evaluations.

At the conclusion of the interview, the parents should know specifically:

— What the child is able to do in reading.

— What the next steps of progress will be.

— How the parents can help to achieve this progress.

Further interviews with parents should be held at regular times throughout the school year, and the records kept in the "Individual Reading Profile" should be shared with the parents.

At the conclusion of the school year, a written report is issued to parents. It should contain feedback as to the child's skills, attitudes, and knowledge. It should state what the child can do and give the parents one or two future goals.

• Reporting to parents by the child:

Children at this level are capable of regularly reporting their own progress to their parents.

Children can:

— Share their reading logs with their parents.
— Share their self-evaluation reading form. (See page 22)
— Write a written report about themselves.

Overview of Writing Program
Fluency-plus Stage

Teacher's Targets and Methods		Children's Targets	Monitoring
To establish an interesting, balanced, and enjoyable program:	By Shared Writing, Guided Writing, Independent Writing, Focus Writing, by exposing children to a wide variety of writing genres.	**Process Focus:** To use editing and proofreading skills. To improve the message by rearranging, expanding, adding, or deleting material. To check spelling. To check punctuation. To check grammar. To use references to assist accuracy.	Observations.
To continue to foster a love of writing:	By an enthusiastic approach.		Individual conferences.
To encourage independence:	By allowing children to make their own choices in writing, by encouraging self-editing.	**Product Focus** To be able to plan a story. To write in a number of genres for a variety of audiences and purposes. To be able to write accurate first drafts when the occasion demands. To be aware of the "tools" of writers (for example, imagery) and use these "tools" when appropriate.	Written language samples.
To cater to individual needs:	By regular monitoring of children's writing progress.	To publish in a variety of forms. To confidently share writing with an audience for comment. To write for own pleasure and enjoyment.	
To help children think more clearly, express themselves more adequately, and communicate effectively:	By listening, discussing, conferencing, and sharing writing.	To be able to self-evaluate To understand that writing is an important learning tool in all areas of the school curriculum. To write fluently and accurately with expression.	Writing and Spelling checklists.
		To express more complex ideas. To use appropriate vocabulary in different situations.	Self-evaluation.

Writing

Overview of the Writing Program

The overview consists of four parts:

- The teacher's targets—the aims or objectives.

- The methods—the program used to reach the teacher's targets.

- The children's targets—what the child should achieve at the fluency-plus level.

- Monitoring—the collection of data in a variety of ways.

This overview is at the fluency-plus level. Fluency-plus indicates that the child is an independent, confident, and competent writer. However, all children in the class may not be at this level. They could be at emergent, early, or fluency levels. The overviews for these levels are included in the Sunshine Series *Whole Language Evaluation* (for the primary grades) by Jill Eggleton.

Note: It must be emphasized that it is not the age of the child that determines where the individual writing program begins but where the child is at.

Teachers' Targets

To establish an interesting, balanced, and enjoyable program.

To continue to foster a love of writing.

To encourage independence.

To cater to individual needs.

To help children think more clearly, express themselves more adequately, and communicate effectively.

Methods for Achieving the Targets

1. **Shared Writing**
2. **Guided Writing**
3. **Independent Writing**

1. Shared Writing

In Shared Writing, teachers and children in partnership share the creating and writing process. Sharing with others (by talking or writing about ideas) gives children feedback on whether their ideas have worked or not.

2. Guided Writing

In Guided Writing, a group of children talk and write together with the teacher (or a child) recording.

Guided Writing is used to model writing genres (such as reports, diaries, or poetic forms). Children with similar needs can be grouped for assistance with writing skills (skills such as paragraphing or plotting a story line).

Focus Writing (or modeling)

In Focus Writing, the teacher writes, focusing attention on a particular skill that the children can transfer to their own writing when appropriate. The teacher should model a variety of styles and conventions. The purpose of Focus Writing is to teach writing skills that lead to writing independence.

3. Independent Writing

In Independent Writing, children are responsible for the drafting, editing, and publishing of their written work.

Organization for Independent Writing can be established as follows:

• Establish a "My Writing Record" booklet for each child.

• The writer selects a topic from the writing file in "My Writing Record" to write about.

• The writer drafts the writing.

• The writer (after referring to the Self-evaluation Chart — see page 48) makes any necessary changes to the writing.

• The writer shares the draft with another writer to get "audience" feedback and *constructive* advice.

• The writer conferences with the teacher (who selects one or two teaching points to focus the writer's attention on).

- The writer redrafts the story and edits. Redrafting can be tackled in a group sharing session. The writer reads his story to the group. The group can make positive suggestions about the content. At the end of the session, the writer can decide whether to incorporate these suggestions in another draft or whether to file the draft (as is) in a writing folder. (The draft may still be reworked later when a further idea occurs.)

  Note: The child should edit the writing independently and decide if it is to be published. (Not all writing will be published.)

- If the writing is not published, the writer files it in his/her folder and fills in the appropriate sheet in the writing file.

- If the writing is to be published, the writer conferences with the teacher about the publishing. Together, they work as a team to make sure the final form meets the required standard. At this stage, the teacher will be concerned with the layout and accuracy.

- The writer publishes the piece of writing.

- The writer is given *positive* feedback from his or her own readers. The readers could fill in a "What Do You Think?" response sheet.

What Do You Think?	
Reader's Name	Comment

Note: The importance of a writer being given positive feedback about his or her material must be established. The response sheet and ideas for making helpful comments need to be discussed with the children.

Children's Targets

The following target chart outlines the skills the children should be aiming to acquire at the fluency-plus level.

They are targets that should be encouraged, taught, and reinforced through the variety of reading and writing approaches mentioned in the overviews. They should be developed through the normal class program with reinforcing and re-teaching as the need arises.

CHILDREN'S TARGETS

Process Focus

To use editing skills and proofreading to improve the message by rearranging, expanding, adding, or deleting material.
To check spelling.
To check punctuation.
To check grammar.
To use references to assist accuracy.

Product Focus

To be able to:

— Plan a story.
— Write in a number of genres for a variety of audiences and purposes.
— Write accurate first drafts when the occasion demands.
— Be aware of the "tools" of writers, (for example, imagery), and use these "tools" when appropriate.
— Publish in a variety of forms.
— Write for own pleasure and enjoyment.
— Confidently share writing with an audience for comment.
— Self-evaluate.
— Understand that writing is an important learning tool in all areas of the curriculum.
— Write fluently and accurately with expression.
— Express more complex ideas.
— Use appropriate vocabulary in different situations.

Monitoring Progress

Monitoring is the process of collecting a variety of information that can be used to establish where the child is at and what the next learning steps could be.

In writing, the following methods are used to monitor progress.

1. **Observations**
2. **Individual Conferences**
3. **Written Language Samples**
4. **Writing and Spelling Checklists**
5. **Self-evaluation**

1. Observations

Evaluation of children's writing can best be made by observations over a period of time.

At the beginning of the school year, initial observations should be made. The focus of these observations should be on attitude and interest. For example:

*   Does the child settle quickly to the writing task, readily selecting writing materials?

*   Does the child have a willing attitude toward writing? Can he or she select topics to write on?

*   Does the child show enthusiasm at each stage of the writing process?

*   Is the child keen to share his or her writing with an audience?

Specific notes on these initial observations should be kept in the appropriate space in the children's "Individual Writing and Spelling Profile" (see page 50).

If a "lack of interest" is observed, some intervention by the teacher would be necessary.

Other observations are ongoing throughout the year and should give the teacher an intimate understanding of the child's strengths, needs, and rate of progress. These observations can be gained by individual conferences.

2. Individual Conferences

*   The roving conference:

    The roving conference involves the teacher moving around the classroom, observing children at various writing tasks. It is usual for a teacher to ask questions such as:

    "What are you writing?"

"Where are you at?"

"What are you going to do next?"

A teacher needs to observe children's responses and take note of significant behaviors if necessary.

A roving conference is also an opportunity for a teacher to "slip in" beside a child and give support. Note would be made of any specific strengths or weaknesses observed.

- The individual conference

An individual conference is a conversation between the teacher and child about the writing in progress. It is a time for a teacher to make observational notes that will be helpful in evaluating. These notes are recorded in the conference section of the "Individual Writing and Spelling Profile."

The following organization could form the basis of the individual conference:

— The child reads the piece of writing to the teacher. The teacher observes, analyzing the style, content, organization, and "mechanical" skills evident in the piece.

— The teacher summarizes the piece of writing, indicating to the child what he or she has communicated, and gives the child an opportunity to correct if a wrong message has been conveyed. The teacher asks the child what he or she thinks of the writing. (It helps the child to form an independent judgment if the teacher has withheld reaction to the writing at this stage.)

— The teacher responds to the content of the writing, describing what he or she found interesting, and asks questions regarding detail, organization, and clarity.

— The teacher encourages the child to think about what he or she would do if they wanted to add more information or rearrange, expand, or delete material. How could the piece of writing be improved?

— The teacher reinforces what the child has done correctly (for example, in spelling, punctuation, use of details, organization, and other process skills). It is important that the child is aware of what has been done correctly so that he or she will correctly repeat this in the future.

— The teacher selects one or two learning needs to focus on. (It is usually the need that is the greatest one in terms of clarifying a piece of writing.)

— The teacher encourages the child to think about what he or she will do next with the writing. It can be:

a) Redrafted
    Edited
    Filed

b) Redrafted
    Edited
    Published

If the child elects to publish the writing, he or she should then have an editing conference with the teacher. The focus in this conference will be on correctness and the editing and proofreading skills needed to achieve this.

At the conclusion of the conference, the teacher records in the "Individual Writing and Spelling Profile" (see page 50) specific information regarding the child's strengths and areas of weakness to work on. This information is shared with the child.

3.   Written Language Samples

While there will be many samples of a child's writing in his or her individual writing and spelling file, it is valuable to collect writing samples for closer analysis and to file these in the child's "Individual Writing and Spelling Profile."

When collecting writing samples, no teacher direction or prewriting activities should be given and two samples should be obtained: one for analysis of writing, the other for analysis of proofreading.

Sample 1: Analysis of writing

- Collect from the child a draft written in a prescribed time (for example, thirty minutes) on a topic chosen by the child. Read the piece of writing carefully and complete the first part of the "Analysis of Writing" sheet.

Analysis of Writing
Name .... Age .... Date ....
Writing Analysis
Writes one or two ideas. ☐
Writes several sequential ideas in a simple structure without punctuation. ☐
Writes several sequential ideas with more complex structure and some punctuation. ☐
Writes a story using a sequence of complex sentences correctly punctuated. ☐
Writes a story using a sequence of complex sentences correctly punctuated and with paragraph structure. ☐
Comment:

Sample 2: Analysis of proofreading

- Ask children to write (unassisted) on a topic of their choice. Give the children a set time (for example, ten minutes).

- At the conclusion of the writing time allowed, ask the children to take a colored pen and work on their writing. They can change it in any way that they think could improve the writing. They can use resources in the room (but cannot seek the advice of the teacher or another child). Give the children a set time to complete their proofreading. During this time, observe the classroom resources that are used.

- Examine the writing and fill in the "Analysis of Proofreading" sheet.

Analysis of Proofreading

Name ....Age .... Date ....

Was unable to make any improvements.   ☐

Has recognized a need to change by working on:
- message conveyed   ☐
- sequence   ☐
- grammar   ☐
- punctuation   ☐
- spelling   ☐

Attempted to change by working on:
- message conveyed   ☐
- sequence   ☐
- grammar   ☐
- punctuation   ☐
- spelling   ☐

Was able to improve:
- message conveyed   ☐
- sequence   ☐
- grammar   ☐
- punctuation   ☐
- spelling   ☐

Comment:

Resources used

Wall display ☐   Atlas ☐   Dictionary ☐   Thesaurus ☐
Other reference ☐   No reference used ☐
Child not independent ☐   Child independent ☐

By repeating this type of evaluation throughout the year, change in writing behavior can be assessed. With careful diagnosis of children's writing, the teacher can be assisted in planning for specific individual or group lessons based on children's needs. The children's writing samples are filed in the child's "Individual Writing and Spelling Profile" (see page 51) and the "Analysis of Writing" sheet is attached.

The following are examples of writing samples and completed analysis sheet.

Tuesday   2 July
                                        Andrew Hough
A crockadial   Art
Slowly   the crockadial aproachs the pond, looking closly at his prey (a tree snake). Silently
he sinks under the water not making even the
slitest ripple. He looks at his prey with a
blood thirsty look then disappeareds under the
shiny surface. Right under his dinner he gets
ready for the pounce!. Then Wham!!! the teeth
of the crockadial are into the snake like
the carving knife in the roast. He thrashes the
snake in the water wildly trying to kill the
snake. Then he trys to drown his prey, so he takes
a big breath then dives under the water. After a
while he comes up with a face of victory,
the snake is dead now and the crockadial
takes it and berries it on the bank. When the
body of the snake decomposes the crockadile
will come back and eat it.

Red   Head   the dragon
Once there was a fierce dragon called
                    fierce
Red Head the dragon he could blow fire
and scare away any knight who challen-
                                        challenge
ged him to a duel. He went around everda-
y looking for Castles to attack, after he
attacked each castle he would runaway
with the castles treasure all the lords and
                                        Lords
Kings feared Red Head and ordered all
there knights to guard there priceless
treasures. But it didn't matter how heav ely
                                        heavily
guarded it was it wasn't good enough red head could steel anything he wanted.
Andrew

Analysis of Writing

Name ..*Andrew*.. Age *9.0*......... Date ..*2.7*...............

1. Writing Analysis

☐	Writes one or two ideas.
☐	Writes several sequential ideas in a simple structure without punctuation.
☐	Writes several sequential ideas with more complex structure and some punctuation.
✓	Writes a story using a sequence of complex sentences correctly punctuated.
☐	Writes a story using a sequence of complex sentences correctly punctuated and with paragraph structure

Comment:

Clear message—very good imagery—uses descriptive words well. Needs to think about paragraphing.

2. Analysis of Proofreading

Has recognized a need to change by working on:

message conveyed	☐
grammar	☐
punctuation	☐
spelling	✓

Attempted to change by working on:

message	☐
grammar	☐
punctuation	☐
spelling	✓

Was able to improve:

message	☐
grammar	☐
punctuation	☐
spelling	✓

Was unable to make any improvements.   ☐

Comment:

Andrew is recognizing a need to change spelling and has worked on improving this. Needs to focus proofreading now on improving punctuation and message. While the message is clear, he will still need to try and add, alter or delete.

Resources used

Wall display	✓	Dictionary	✓	Atlas	☐
Thesaurus		Other	✓	No reference	
Child not independent	☐	Child independent	✓	used	

4. Writing and Spelling Checklists

Checklists can provide a sound organizational structure for gathering information for evaluation purposes.

They are individual checklists of competencies kept by the teacher in the child's "Individual Writing and Spelling Profile." They incorporate main skills for the child to aim at and achieve—according to his or her particular level. (Note: Skills to aim at will vary according to the needs.)

Writing Checklists can be filled in after observation, conferencing, or analysis of a written language sample.

It should be noted that if checklists are used, the items being checked must be worth evaluating. If there is no sound educational reason for recording information, we need not bother.

The following is an example of a writing checklist at the fluency-plus stage of writing. It must be noted that spelling forms an integrated part of the writing process and therefore the one checklist is designed to cover both.

Writing and Spelling Checklist		
Spelling	**Written language— Stage: fluency-plus**	**Date & comment if necessary**
Has understanding of spelling generalizations (e.g., q and u, plurals, silent e, ie and ei, final consonants, words ending -y and words ending -ful).		
Uses dictionary skills. Uses a thesaurus. Uses an atlas.		
	Process Focus: • Uses editing and proofreading skills to improve the message by rearranging, expanding, adding, or deleting material. • Uses editing skills to: — check spelling. — check punctuation. — check grammar.	
	Product Focus: • Writes in a number of genres for a variety of audiences and purposes (e.g., speeches, plays, reports, diaries). • Publishes in a variety of forms. • Writes for own pleasure. • Writes accurate first drafts when the occasion demands.	

5.   Self-evaluation

Self-evaluation is the most significant kind of evaluation. As the child evaluates his or her own learning, involvement in that learning increases.

In written language, children should be encouraged to reflect on their own writing and establish what they could do to improve their writing. They should assume the role of the reader or the editor. Each learner must discover reading strategies that allow him or her to be a successful language user.

The following are some suggestions to encourage children in self-evaluation.

• Each child could have a "Self-evaluation Chart" that they could refer to as they work through the various stages of the writing process.

Self-evaluation Chart

Before writing, ask yourself...

• Have I decided why I am doing this piece of writing?
• Have I decided who is my audience?
• Have I decided what I want my audience to know after reading this writing?
• Have I decided what I want my reader to feel?
• Have I decided whether I need to gather any information before I begin?
• Have I decided how I will begin?

After the first draft, ask yourself...

• Have I said what I wanted to say?
• Is there anything I should take out?
• Is there anything I could add?
• Will the beginning grab the reader's attention?
• Have I used the best words I can?
• Will the readers feel what I want them to feel?
• Have I ended the writing well?
• Are my ideas in a sensible order?
• Have I put things that go together in a paragraph?

Before the final draft, ask yourself...

• Have I used correct punctuation?
• Have I left out any words?
• Have I used paragraphs?
• Are there any words I need to check for correct spelling?
• How will I make my writing attractive to the reader?

- Get the children to fill in the "What have I learned about writing?" and "What can I do to help myself?" charts in the "My Writing Record" booklet.

- The children can write their own report to share with their teacher and parents.

Example:

```
┌──────────────────────────────────────────────────────────────────────┐
│                                                                        │
│  Written language report on .........................................  │
│                                                                        │
│  Things I can do well:                                                 │
│                                                                        │
│                                                                        │
│  Things I want to learn:                                               │
│                                                                        │
│                                                                        │
│                                                                        │
│  Signed ..............................................................  │
│                                                                        │
└──────────────────────────────────────────────────────────────────────┘
```

The "Individual Writing and Spelling Profile"

Information about the child's writing needs to be collated in a way that makes it easily accessible to the teacher and parents. An "Individual Writing and Spelling Profile" can be established for each individual. This profile should contain background information about the child, observation notes, language samples, conference notes, writing and spelling checklists, and relevant parent comments.

It is a permanent record that can be used for:

— Sharing with parents during interviews.
— Writing written reports for parents.
— Sharing with the child.
— Gaining specific information for the Cumulative Record Card. (See page 29)

The "Individual Writing and Spelling Profile".

The following pages outline the format of the "Individual Writing and Spelling Profile."

Individual Writing and Spelling Profile: Page One   Individual Writing and Spelling Profile: Page Two

Writing and Spelling Profile

Name:

Background information:

Informal observations:
(Date and record any informal observations that are relevant.)

Formal writing observations:
(Record observations for a specific purpose, such as interest, attitude.)

Date	Teacher action

Conference notes:
(After conferencing with child, date and record relevant, specific information.)

Parent comments:
(Record any relevant comments by parents during interviews or at other times.)

Language samples:
(Attach language samples taken throughout the year.)

Using the Data

The data collected from observations, writing samples, individual conferences, and writing checklists can be used in the following ways:

1. **Evaluating Children's Progress**
   (to give children information about their progress)

2. **Evaluating the Program**
   (to give teachers information about the effectiveness of their program)

3. **Reporting to Parents**

1. **Evaluating Children's Progress**

   Children's progress should be evaluated to give them feedback that will facilitate learning.

   Children should understand how their progress is measured and how to use the feedback of the evaluation. Teachers should share the "Individual Writing and Spelling Profile" with each individual. Using the data gathered in the monitoring process, the teacher should:

   • Diagnose the child's difficulties and give a lead as to how he or she might improve.

   • Motivate the child to learn further.

   • Encourage the child toward self-evaluation.

2. **Evaluating the Program**

   Evaluation should involve judgements about the writing program as well as about children's progress. It is an essential link between learning and planning for further teaching.

   Teachers should consider their own targets and their children's targets to determine the following:

   • Is the program balanced?

   • Are the children writing and publishing in a variety of ways?

   • Do the children demonstrate a real interest in writing and sharing their work with an audience?

   • Do the children understand the writing process and are they becoming independent at all stages of the process?

- What new aims and objectives need to be set for the next steps in learning?

- What ways do we (as teachers) need to identify our own strengths and recognize skills to develop in order to make the writing program even better?

3. Reporting to Parents

Outline the writing program by newsletter. Give parents an opportunity to participate in, support, and respond to the writing program.

Dear Parents,

The staff of (.........................) welcome you as a parent and look forward to a pleasurable association with you.

We would like to share some positive ways you could help your child continue in his or her written language development.

Our purpose in written language is to provide a program that is enjoyable and that exposes children to a wide variety of different writing styles. Throughout the program, we will be encouraging children to experiment with these styles. They will be editing, proofreading, and publishing their own work and sharing their writing with others.

As parents, your support and encouragement will help develop a positive attitude toward writing.

Your child will be bringing home his or her published stories to share with you. There will be an attached sheet so that you can make positive comments about his or her writing.

You may like to ask your child what he or she feels about the writing and how to improve it next time. Sometimes children need ideas about topics to write on. Your help here would be appreciated.

Our aim is to provide a happy, caring environment with each child actively involved in the learning process.

Please do not compare one child with another. They are all individuals and progress at their own rate.

We would be pleased to discuss any problems or queries that you may have. The education of your child is a partnership.

Yours sincerely,

- After approximately one month of the school year, arrange a parent/teacher discussion to share information about the child and to gain an insight into the child's home attitude toward writing. Record any relevant information in the "Individual Writing and Spelling Profile.". (See page 51)

- After approximately three months of the school year, a formal interview between teacher and parent is arranged. This is the time for the teacher to formally share with the parents the child's achievements to date and to outline future goals.

  The teacher will use the data gathered from:

  — Observations.
  — Language samples.
  — Conference notes.
  — Checklists.
  — Self-evaluation.

  At the conclusion of the interview, the parents should know specifically the writing skills that the child has achieved and his or her understanding of the process, what the further goals will be, and how parents can help their child achieve these.

- At regular times throughout the school year, interviews with parents should be held. These interviews should show parents what their child can do now and compare the progress since the last interview.

- At all times, the records kept in the "Individual Writing and Spelling Profile" should be shared with the parents. At the conclusion of the school year (or on a more regular basis as desired by school and parents), a written report is issued to parents.

Reports should:

— Focus on the learning achievements of the individual child.
— Describe the knowledge, skills, attitudes, and values being developed.
— Be in sufficient detail for the parents to feel confident that the report informs them about the learning that has occurred.
— Be frequent and meaningful.
— Give opportunities for parents to share information about their child.
— Give parents one or two ideas about future goals.

Children should be encouraged to report to parents regularly on their own progress. This reporting could be done by sharing their writing files with their parents, sharing their published stories, sharing their self-evaluation report form, or writing a full report on how they see themselves as writers.

Overview of Spelling Program
Fluency-plus Stage

Teacher's Targets and Method		Children's Targets	Monitoring
To develop a positive attitude toward spelling:	By having an accepting supportive learning environment that encourages children to write.	To have a "spelling conscience." To show a positive attitude toward spelling.	Observations.
To use a variety of approaches to teach spelling:	By teaching sound-symbol relationships, visual and sound patterns, and the meaning base of words and using words in context.	To be able to edit and proofread their own writing with increasing accuracy.	Written language samples to analyze spelling strategies.
To encourage independence in proofreading and editing:	By encouraging children to be responsible for editing, proofreading, and publishing their own work.	To be independent in locating the conventional spelling of words.	
To encourage children to use a variety of spelling references (for example, dictionaries, a thesaurus, an atlas):	By providing a variety of modern references and having a print-rich environment.	To be able to use accurately a variety of references.	Writing and Spelling checklists.
To teach or maintain specific, useful generali-zations of spelling:	By introducing or reinforcing the useful generalizations of spelling through the daily reading and writing program.	To understand specific skills and generalizations of spelling and apply them in personal writing. To learn the conventional spelling of common words used in everyday writing.	Self-evaluation.
To extend and enrich children's vocabulary:	By experimentation with word building, word analysis, word meaning, word origins, and word usage through reading and writing experiences.	To increase word knowledge.	
To develop in children a spelling conscience and to assist them to learn to spell accurately the common words used in everyday writing:	By encouraging children to locate their own errors in their written work, and encouraging them to develop a learning method that best suits them.		

Spelling

Overview of the Spelling Program

The evaluation of a child's ability to spell should be based on how well he or she spells in his or her written language.

Spelling is a tool of written language and not an end in itself. It should be viewed in the context of writing and not as an isolated skill.

The teaching of spelling should relate to the child's interests and experiences. Emphasis should be placed on developing skills related to the uses, meanings and structures of words rather than on developing the skill of reproducing letters in a conventional sequence.

It is important to build the right attitude toward spelling. Children need to know that correct spelling is a courtesy to a reader and that the writing is not finished until the message is written correctly. They need to know, however, that everyone makes mistakes, that in first drafts this is acceptable and that they can be corrected during proofreading.

There are many ways that children learn to spell, so it is important to use a variety of approaches in a class program.

Children should be taught:

— Sound-symbol relationships in spelling. This gives them a basic strategy to use. They need to know that sounds relate to written symbols. It is important, however, not to overstress phonic rules.

— Visual and sound patterns in spelling. Encourage the child to ask "Does it look right?" "Does it sound right?"

— The meaning base of words. Talk with children about roots and affixes of words.

— The fact that words must be used in context.

The essential elements of a spelling program are:

1. Vocabulary Extension and Enrichment
2. The Development of Understanding about Spelling Generalizations
3. Word Learning

1. **Vocabulary Extension and Enrichment**

Vocabulary extension and enrichment should form a natural, integrated part of the daily reading and writing programs.

These programs will provide many opportunities to extend and reinforce children's vocabulary knowledge. Vocabulary extension and enrichment could consist of:

- Word building.
- Word analysis.
- Word meanings.
- Word origins.
- Word usage.

2. **The Development of Understanding about Spelling Generalizations**

There is a place for some study of spelling generalizations. Competent spellers can be given the task of discussing just how "general" the rules are.

This study should be introduced and reinforced as the words occur in context.

Children should be encouraged to make notes independently in the "My Spelling Record" booklet of any spelling generalizations they know or would like to remember (generalizations—or rules— that they have worked out for themselves and which work for them).

3. **Word Learning**

At the fluency-plus stage, the encouragement of a good attitude to spelling should continue to be fostered. Children at the fluency-plus level of spelling would, most likely, be making very few personal errors in their written work. It is, however, important that children continue to appreciate that correct spelling is worthwhile and that their writing is not complete until all errors have been corrected.

Words for learning should be words relating to the child's interest and experience. They should be words he or she has used in context and had some difficulty in spelling correctly.

The steps for word learning can be as follows:

- The child edits and proofreads his or her written work by underlining all errors.

- The child uses word references to find the correct spelling and writes the correct version above his or her attempt.

- The child and/or teacher selects words from these corrected errors to enter in the word bank in the "My Spelling Record" booklet.

- The child selects words from the word bank to "bring to fluency."

Children will discover how they best learn words that they have misspelled. Responsibility in forming their own word-learning strategies needs to be encouraged. The learning needs to be meaningful and enjoyable to the individual.

The following are some useful ideas for word-learning strategies.

- Cut the letters out of magazines or newspapers and arrange them in a variety of ways to form the word.

- Write the word using as many different printing styles as possible.

- Write the word using a variety of media, for example calligraphic pens, felt-tip pens or glitter pens.

- Type the word using different fonts on a computer (if a computer is available).

Monitoring Progress

The initiation of good spelling skills requires careful monitoring of each child's development.

In spelling, the following methods are used to monitor:

1. **Observations**
2. **Written Language Samples to Analyze Spelling Strategies**
3. **Writing and Spelling Checklist**
4. **Self-evaluation**

1. **Observations**

    It is important that the teacher observes the child's attitude toward spelling and diagnoses specific spelling problems through careful observation of the types of error being made by the child.

    For example:

    - Does the child have a poor visual memory for certain letter patterns?

    - Are there any patterns in the spelling errors the child is making?

    - Is the child independent in using various references to locate words?

    - Can the child retain in memory a specific spelling generalization and apply it in his or her written work?

- Has the child a positive attitude toward spelling (evident by the development of a "spelling conscience"), and does he or she incorporate care and accuracy in work?

- Is the child developing an enriched vocabulary?

Specific notes on these observations should be kept in the appropriate space in the child's "Individual Writing and Spelling Profile." (See page 50.)

2. Written Language Samples to Analyze Spelling Strategies

Written language samples can be used to diagnose more specifically the child's spelling strategies and to determine what his or her needs are.

When children make an error in their writing, analyzing the errors helps teachers to gain an insight into how children are applying their base of understandings. Even "spellers" having difficulties are working from some "understanding base." By analyzing children's spelling errors, a teacher can discover what this "base" is.

To analyze a child's spelling strategies:

- Use a writing sample. Children should be given time to proofread their work first. This assists accurate diagnosis.

- Observe the spelling strategies used and fill in the spelling analysis sheet.

- Share with the child the results of the analysis and plan specific individual or group lessons based on each child's needs.

Note: By repeating this type of evaluation throughout the year, change in spelling behavior can be assessed.

Dale

The Spooky castle
~~Ones~~ once ~~abown~~ upon a time ~~they~~ there was a
Spooky castle on top of a Spooky
hall. One day ~~theys~~ these three ~~man~~ men
came to look for a ~~gop~~ job. They became
~~Svents~~ sevants. ~~Thes~~ These boys said, I am
looking for a pleas to saty the
nihy. I said you have came to
the ranty plase. I told one of
my ~~Svents~~.

Spelling Analysis Sheet

Name .....Dale...

Spelling analysis

- Has proofread for spelling errors ✓
- Has used word sources to locate errors ✓

Took time to do this. Tended to rely on another child as he found looking up the dictionary time-consuming.

- Has consistently made the following types of errors:
  confusion between a   u
                   g   j
                 c   s

- Has applied the following rules and generalizations:
  added "ing"

Comment:
Confusion with vowel sounds. Has used precisely "sound-symbol relationship" for initial letter and most initial blends. Needs to focus on visual patterns.

3. Writing and Spelling Checklists

These are individual checklists of competencies kept by the teacher in the child's "Individual Writing and Spelling Profile."

They incorporate main skills to be achieved by children at this level. Skills will vary according to the needs of each class. These checklists can be marked after observations, conferences, or written language samples have been done.

For the "Writing and Spelling Checklist," see page 47.

4. Self-evaluation

In self-evaluation, the child evaluates his or her own learning and sets new goals. Children are natural evaluators. They learn both from their errors and their successful accomplishments. Children should be encouraged to reflect on their spelling, analyze it, and then use their analysis to improve their work.

They could ask themselves:

• Can I locate errors myself and correct them?

• Can I remember some spelling generalizations and use them in my writing?

• Am I learning new words and using them?

• Am I remembering the correct spelling of some words I had difficulty with?

The following are some suggestions to encourage children in self-evaluation.

a) Ask the children to fill in the chart "Have I" on page 15 of the "My Spelling Record" booklet. (This could be done each week.)

b) The children can write their own spelling reports to their parents.

Spelling report on:

Things I can do well:

Things I want to learn:

Signed:..

c) The children could fill in their own Spelling Analysis Sheet and attach it to a writing sample.

Using the Data

The data collected in observations, language samples, and the "Writing and Spelling Checklists" is used in the following ways:

1. **Evaluating Children's Progress**
   (to give children information about their progress)

2. **Evaluating the Program**
   (to give teachers information about the effectiveness of their program.)

3. **Reporting to Parents**

1. **Evaluating Children's Progress**

   Children's progress should be evaluated to give feedback that will facilitate their learning. Children should understand how progress is measured and how to use the feedback.

   Using the data gathered in the monitoring process, the teacher should:

   • Understand what is being measured.

   • Diagnose each child's difficulties and give him or her a lead as to how he might improve.

   • Motivate the child to further learning.

   • Lead the child toward self-evaluation.

   • Share the "Individual Writing and Spelling Profile" with each individual.

2. **Evaluating the Program**

   Evaluation should involve judgments about the spelling program as well as about pupil's progress. It is an essential link between learning and planning for further teaching.

   In evaluating the program, teachers should consider their own targets and their children's targets to define the following:

   • Have the children developed a positive attitude toward spelling?

   • Are they able to make confident attempts at spelling all words?

- Are they independently using proofreading and editing skills?

- Is there time given to word enrichment and generalizations of spelling?

- Are the spelling resources up-to-date and varied?

- Is there a print-saturated environment?

- Do children show an interest in words—their meanings and origins?

- What still needs to be learned and what new aims and objectives need to be set for the next steps in learning?

- In what ways do we, as teachers, need to develop our own strengths and recognize skills to develop in order to make the spelling program even better?

By reflecting upon the information collected, analyzing it, and using it, a teacher will provide for growth and development within his or her program.

3. **Reporting to Parents**

The same guidelines as established for reading and written language should be followed for spelling.

In reporting to parents on spelling, the following specific suggestions are made:

- Outline the spelling program in a newsletter (or parent meeting). Give parents an opportunity to respond to the program and share their thoughts.

Dear Parents,

Your child is becoming an independent speller.

Our purpose is to develop a positive attitude toward spelling, and we would like you to help us in this endeavor.

The spelling program is closely related to the reading and writing programs.

Spelling is not just learning words. In our spelling program, we want to extend and enrich children's vocabulary, to help them use word sources that are available, to show them (through reading and writing) some general rules that apply to spelling, to lead them toward independence in proofreading and editing, and to encourage them to retain the conventional spelling of some errors that they may have made in their written language.

Most children will make errors in their written work. Our purpose is not to discourage this but rather to show them how to proofread and where to find the correct spelling, and to give them ideas as to how they could learn the word.

Your child will have a word bank. This word bank will contain words that he or she has used in written language and can *almost* spell!. It is not intended that he or she should write these words out again and again. This does not ensure that the words will be learned. The learning of these words should be enjoyable and meaningful.

The following are some ways that could help your child to retain the conventional spelling.

- Ask your child to find the letters of the word in magazines or newspapers. Cut them out and rearrange them.

- Ask your child to write the word, using as many different printing styles as possible.

- Ask your child to experiment with a variety of media (e.g., calligraphic pens, felt-tip, glitter pens).

- Ask your child to use a computer (if available) to type the word using a variety of fonts.

Your child will not be tested on these words in a formal way. The true test is whether next time, when he or she needs to use these words in written work, he or she can recall the conventional spelling.

Some children find it difficult to retain the correct spelling of words. Our purpose is to teach them the importance of using word sources to confirm and check spellings before any work is published for an audience.

Other ways you can help encourage your child's interest in words are:

Playing word games (e.g., Scrabble ®).
Pointing out unusual words.
Pointing out differences and similarities in words.
Discussing the meaning of words seen or used.
Discussing rules that apply to the spelling of some words.

We hope to have an accepting and supporting learning environment where children extend their knowledge of words in a natural and positive way.

Yours sincerely,

- After one month of the school year, arrange a parent/teacher discussion to share information about the child with the teacher and to gain an insight into the child's home attitude toward spelling. Record any relevant information in the "Individual Writing and Spelling Profile." (See page 51)

- After three months of the school year, a formal interview between teacher and parents is arranged. This is the time for the teacher to share with the parents the child's achievements to date and to outline future goals. The teacher will use the data gathered from:

  — Observations.
  — Language samples.
  — Conference notes.
  — Checklists.
  — Self-evaluation.

At the conclusion of the interview, the parents should know the spelling strengths or weaknesses of the child, what the future goals will be, and how they can help their child achieve these.

At regular times throughout the school year, interviews with parents should be held. These interviews should show parents what their child can do now and compare the progress since the last interview. The records kept in the "Individual Writing and Spelling Profile" should be shared.

At the conclusion of the school year (or more frequently, if required), a written report is issued to parents.

Reports should:

— Focus on the learning achievements of the individual child.
— Describe the knowledge, skills, attitudes, and values being developed.
— Be in sufficient detail for the parents to feel confident that the report informs them about the learning that has occurred.
— Be frequent and meaningful.
— Give opportunities for parents to share information about their child.
— Give the parents one or two ideas about future goals.

Children should be encouraged to report to their parents regularly on their own progress. This reporting could be done by sharing their "Individual Writing and Spelling Profiles" with parents, sharing their self-evaluation chart (that indicates "Things I Can Do Well") or writing a full report on how they see themselves as spellers.

What to Do with the Data

Information about the child's spelling needs to be collated in a way that makes it easily accessible to the teacher and parents.

An "Individual Writing and Spelling Profile" can be established for each child. (See page 50.) It should contain background information about the child, observation notes, writing and spelling checklists, and relevant parent comments. It is a permanent record that can be used for:

— Sharing with parents during parent interviews.
— Writing written reports for parents.
— Sharing with the child.
— Gaining specific information for cumulative record cards. (See page 29.)

Monitoring Timetable

Monitoring is ongoing and an integral part of the class program.

A timetable to assist teachers in the classroom organization of monitoring is essential. A monitoring timetable establishes a system whereby teachers need only to focus on one area to be monitored each week. (Naturally, there are some areas requiring ongoing monitoring that cannot simply be slotted into a weekly time slot.)

The monitoring timetable is organized into an eight-week block. After eight weeks, the timetable is repeated. It should be emphasized that the areas to be monitored form part of the normal class program.   For example, written language samples should be taken as part of the written language program and running records should be taken in reading time.

Observations and running records have been given a two-week time slot due to the time involved in these records.

MONITORING TIMETABLE		
WEEK	METHODS OF DATA GATHERING	ONGOING DATA GATHERING
1	Observations for specific purpose.	Observations
2	Observations for specific purpose.	
3	Running records.	Conferences
4	Running records.	Self-evaluation
5	Language samples for proofreading analysis, writing analysis, spelling analysis.	
6	Language samples for proofreading analysis, writing analysis, spelling analysis.	
7	Running records.	
8	Running records.	

Conclusion

Evaluation is an integral part of a whole-language program. It is a process of observing, collecting information, reflecting, analyzing, and using this information to work with children and parents.

An effective evaluation program evolves around the following criteria:

- The formulation of a school statement on evaluation.

- The preparation for each child of:

  a)   An "Individual Reading Profile."

  b)   An "Individual Writing and Spelling Profile."

  c)   A Cumulative Record Card.

- The preparation of a monitoring timetable.

- The use of the data gathered to give information to children about their progress.

- The process of sharing formally and informally with parents the class program in reading, writing, and spelling.

- The establishment of a written report form that is not comparative but reflects what the child is able to do.

- The continual evaluation of the class program to ensure that it is effectively meeting the needs of individual children.

Evaluation should assist teachers in determining where the child is in growth and development and provide a springboard for the next steps in learning.

Running Record Resource

The following section contains running record sheets that can be photocopied for classroom use. Teachers can use this resource to establish the level at which a child can read competently by selecting a running record sheet that they think a child can read and subsequently moving up or down the levels as needed. (For a full description of how to use running records, see page 16)

The running record sheets in this section have been based on text from the following Sunshine books:

Volcanoes (Sunshine, Fact and Fantasy, Level 3)

Crocodile! Crocodile! (Sunshine, Level 6)

The Number Cruncher (Sunshine, Fact and Fantasy, Level 6)

Animals and Air (Sunshine, Fact and Fantasy, Level 6)

The Emperor Penguin (Sunshine, Fact and Fantasy, Level 7)

No Place Like Home (Sunshine, Fact and Fantasy, Level 7)

The Funny, Funny Clown Face (Sunshine, Level 8)

Princess Harimau and the Tiger (Sunshine, Level 8)

Agatha's Brew (Sunshine, Level 9)

Mr. Rumfitt (Sunshine, Level 9)

The Best Diver in the World (Sunshine, Level 10)

Tai Taylor Goes to School (Sunshine, Level 10)

The Haunting of Miss Cardamon (Sunshine, Level 11)

The Stranger from the Sea (Sunshine, Level 11)

Animals at Work (Sunshine, Fact and Fantasy, Level 11)

Running Record Sheet

Name: Age: Date:

E	SC	E M S V	SC M S

Volcanoes (Sunshine, Level 3) 7 to 8 years

Volcanoes erupt. Volcanoes spit out hot rocks.

They hiss out gases. Rumbling and grumbling,

they empty out their crater.

When volcanoes erupt, steam, gases and rocks

are pushed up from deep inside the earth.

It is very hot in the middle of the earth.

Volcanoes can erupt at any time, spitting out melted

rock called lava. Lava is so hot it boils out of the

crater and flows down the slopes of the volcano.

Young volcanoes erupt many times as they grow up.

They often have a beautiful, sloping shape, like an

upside down cone or a funnel.

Sometimes a little volcano grows on the side of a

young volcano.

M = Meaning = Does it make sense?
S = Structure = Does it sound right?
V = Visual = Does it look right?

Write MSV in the appropriate column and circle the type of cue the child has used.

72

Running Record Sheet

Name: Age: Date:

E	SC	E M S V	SC M S

It smokes and puffs like the bigger one.

They can both erupt.

Older volcanoes may be huge mountains.

They have erupted many many times.

These volcanoes still erupt but not so often.

They are dormant, or sleeping.

Very very old volcanoes don't erupt any more.

They are extinct. They look like old mountains.

No more hot rocks, steam or gas is left under extinct

volcanoes.

Volcanoes that still erupt are called active volcanoes,

and they are dangerous.

The rocks they throw out may hit houses and people

many miles away.

M = Meaning = Does it make sense?
S = Structure = Does it sound right?
V = Visual = Does it look right?

Write MSV in the appropriate column and circle the type of cue the child has used.

(198 running words)

Running Record Sheet

Name: Age: Date:

Crocodile! Crocodile! (Sunshine, Level 6) 7 to 8 years

There was once a crocodile who lived in the middle of

a deep, dark, dismal, dripping swamp. For years, he had

lived on nothing but swamp fish.

"I'm sick of swamp fish," the crocodile said one day.

"Other crocodiles eat all sorts of things. I shall go to

town and eat everyone I catch. After all, I am a very,

very, very fierce crocodile with crocodile teeth and

crocodile claws."

The crocodile crawled out of the swamp and under a

hedge and across a lawn. He surprised Mr. Pye, who

was resting in his deck chair reading the paper.

Mr. Pye leaped up and ran away, his green scarf flapping

in the wind behind him.

E	SC	E M S V	SC M S

M = Meaning = Does it make sense?
S = Structure = Does it sound right?
V = Visual = Does it look right?

Write MSV in the appropriate
column and circle the type
of cue the child has used.

Running Record Sheet

Name: Age: Date:

Analysis

E	SC	E M S V	SC M S

As the happy crocodile ate the deck chair and the paper,

he could hear Mr. Pye calling,

"Crocodile! Crocodile!

Here comes the crocodile!"

Then the crocodile climbed over a wall into the main

street of the town.

In front of the post office stood two mail carriers with two

bags of letters. Mail carriers are very brave, but when

they saw the crocodile coming, they were terrified.

They ran away at once.

As the crocodile ate the two bags of letters, he could

hear the mail carriers calling,

"Crocodile! Crocodile!

Here comes the crocodile!"

M = Meaning = Does it make sense?
S = Structure = Does it sound right?
V = Visual = Does it look right?

Write MSV in the appropriate
column and circle the type
of cue the child has used.

(210 running words)

75

Running Record Sheet

Name: Age: Date:

The Number Cruncher (Sunshine, Level 6) 7 to 8 years

E	SC	E M S V	SC M S

Jamie loved getting birthday presents from his

grandfather. It was exciting to wonder what Grandpa

would come up with. He was always inventing clever

gadgets and machines. Jamie's room was full of them.

On his seventh birthday, Jamie's grandfather gave him

a tiny calculator. It was oblong and nearly as thin as

a piece of paper.

When Jamie pushed the on button, the words

Number Cruncher glowed on the small screen.

"Thanks, Grandpa," said Jamie. "But what does a

number cruncher do?"

"I'll let the number cruncher surprise you," Grandpa said.

"It is rather special."

M = Meaning = Does it make sense?
S = Structure = Does it sound right?
V = Visual = Does it look right?

Write MSV in the appropriate
column and circle the type
of cue the child has used.

Running Record Sheet

Name: Age: Date:

Analysis

E	SC	E M S V	SC M S

When Jamie went to bed that night, he put the

number cruncher in his pajama pocket.

He fell asleep right away. It was very late when the

cat jumped up onto his bed and woke him.

He mumbled to himself, "I wonder what the time is?"

In the dark, a squeaky voice said,

"It's twelve-thirty."

"Who said that?" asked Jamie.

"I did," said the squeaky voice from his pocket.

Jamie pulled out his number cruncher.

The numbers 12:30 glowed in the dark.

"You can talk," whispered Jamie.

"Yes," said the squeaky voice, "but only you can hear

me. I can do anything with numbers.

I am your very own number cruncher."

M = Meaning = Does it make sense?
S = Structure = Does it sound right?
V = Visual = Does it look right?

Write MSV in the appropriate
column and circle the type
of cue the child has used.

(206 running words)

Running Record Sheet

Name: Age: Date:

E	SC	E M S V	SC M S

Animals and Air (Sunshine, Level 6) 7 to 8 years

Every moment of every day we breathe air.

When we are awake, asleep, playing, or watching TV,

we breathe air. We breathe air in through our nose and

mouth and into our lungs.

Our lungs absorb (or take) from the air the oxygen that

we need to live, and we breathe out the rest.

Living things all breathe in air.

Giraffes, horses, cows, cats, and dogs all have lungs

like ours. But many animals breathe differently.

Slugs and snails have breathing holes in their sides.

The holes open and shut as they breathe air.

From the air, slugs and snails absorb the oxygen they

need to live and breathe out the rest.

M = Meaning = Does it make sense?
S = Structure = Does it sound right?
V = Visual = Does it look right?

Write MSV in the appropriate
column and circle the type
of cue the child has used.

Running Record Sheet

Name: Age: Date:

Analysis

E	SC	E M S V	SC M S

Worms breathe, too. Through their soft, moist skin,

they absorb water which has oxygen in it.

Spiders breathe air through special openings

underneath their bodies. These special book lungs

absorb the oxygen. Water spiders breathe air, too.

They may come out of the water to get air.

Some water spiders build a silken trap in the water

and fill it with air to breathe.

Fish have noses and nostrils — but not for breathing.

Fish gulp water in through their mouths.

The water goes over feathery gills that absorb the

oxygen from the water.

M = Meaning = Does it make sense?
S = Structure = Does it sound right?
V = Visual = Does it look right?

Write MSV in the appropriate
column and circle the type
of cue the child has used.

(206 running words)

Running Record Sheet

Name: Age: Date:

The Emperor Penguin (Sunshine, Level 7)
7-1/2 to 8-1/2 years

E	SC	E M S V	SC M S

Antarctica, a desert of ice surrounded by stormy seas,

is home to millions of penguins. Among them are the

emperors—the largest penguins of all.

Unlike other penguins, they breed in the harsh

Antarctic winter, when the seas are frozen and the

sun never rises.

Like all penguins, the emperors are rather awkward

on land. They are slow walkers. They waddle along—

their squat bodies swaying and flippers stuck out

to balance them. To speed things up, they often slide

on their bellies down the icy slopes.

Penguins cannot fly. Their wings are too short and

stumpy. But in the water, the emperors, like all penguins,

are completely at home—swimming fast and diving

M = Meaning = Does it make sense?
S = Structure = Does it sound right?
V = Visual = Does it look right?

Write MSV in the appropriate
column and circle the type
of cue the child has used.

Running Record Sheet

Name: Age: Date:

E	SC	E M S V	SC M S

deep to catch food.

Their flippers whirr through the water like small paddle

wheels, and they steer with their outstretched feet

and tails.

Penguins are well protected against the cold.

Their feather coats are both windproof and waterproof.

And a thick layer of fat beneath the skin also helps

keep them warm. Nevertheless, they must band

together in large groups to keep warm during the

winter blizzards.

When the sea ice begins to freeze in March, the

emperors waddle in single file to their breeding grounds.

Each one returns to the exact spot where last year's egg

was laid and calls for its mate.

Penguins know each other's voices well.

M = Meaning = Does it make sense?
S = Structure = Does it sound right?
V = Visual = Does it look right?

Write MSV in the appropriate
column and circle the type
of cue the child has used.

(224 running words)

Running Record Sheet

Name: Age: Date:

No Place Like Home (Sunshine, Level 7)
7-1/2 to 8-1/2 years

E	SC	E M S V	SC M S

"There is no room for hot air balloons in bedrooms,"

said Tom's and Jessie's mother.

"Take that balloon outside!"

"We can never do what we like in our room,"

Tom grumbled. "I think I would like to live somewhere

else."

So Tom and Jessie fired up their balloon and floated

away.

The balloon floated on and on. But at last Tom and

Jessie landed in Lapland on a plain of ice and snow.

There were people on skis lassoing a runaway reindeer.

"We are taking our herd home for the winter," a boy

explained. "We make clothes from reindeer hides.

M = Meaning = Does it make sense?
S = Structure = Does it sound right?
V = Visual = Does it look right?

Write MSV in the appropriate
column and circle the type
of cue the child has used.

Running Record Sheet

Name: Age: Date:

Analysis

E	SC	E M S V	SC M S

We drink reindeer milk and eat their meat."

Tom and Jessie helped the people pack up their tents

and load them onto the sledges.

"In the summer months, we camp in tents by the sea,"

said the boy. "But in the winter we travel inland with

our herds and live in wooden houses, safe and warm."

At their winter home, the people showed Tom and

Jessie how to carve antlers, mend skis, and weave

clothing.

Tom and Jessie helped to collect water through a hole

in the ice.

Their new friend said, "In the winter months, there is

no daylight. We do everything in the dark."

"We would like to stay with you," said Jessie, "but it's

time to fly on."

M = Meaning = Does it make sense?
S = Structure = Does it sound right?
V = Visual = Does it look right?

Write MSV in the appropriate
column and circle the type
of cue the child has used.

(221 running words)

Running Record Sheet

Name: Age: Date:

Analysis

The Funny, Funny Clown Face (Sunshine, Level 8) 8 to 9 years

E	SC	E M S V	SC M S

Gillian's mother gave her a drawing book and some lovely

thick crayons.

First Gillian drew a blue elephant digging with a green spade.

Then she drew a purple kangaroo. Its pouch was full of apples

and cherries. She tried out the black crayon, drawing a funny

squiggly thing, a bit like a man, a bit like a creeping shadow.

Then she drew a whole lot of policemen, all colors of

policemen marching in a rainbow line. Her mother liked all

these drawings.

"What shall I draw next?" she asked her mother.

"Draw a face," said her mother.

Gillian took the red crayon and started to draw.

The face seemed to come out of the crayon all by itself. It made

itself round. It made its smiling mouth smile more at one side

than at the other. It had one big ear and one small ear, but both

sticking out. It had blue eyes and fluffy green hair and a pink

rose instead of a nose.

M = Meaning = Does it make sense?
S = Structure = Does it sound right?
V = Visual = Does it look right?

Write MSV in the appropriate column and circle the type of cue the child has used.

84

Running Record Sheet

Name: Age: Date:

Analysis

E	SC	E M S V	SC M S

Between two tufts of fluffy hair sat a pointed hat, rather like a

wizard's hat, but not so powerful or important. It was not a

wizard's hat or even a wizard's face.

It was a funny, funny clown face.

M = Meaning = Does it make sense?
S = Structure = Does it sound right?
V = Visual = Does it look right?

Write MSV in the appropriate
column and circle the type
of cue the child has used.

(204 running words)

Running Record Sheet

Name: Age: Date:

Princess Harimau and the Tiger (Sunshine, Level 8)
8 to 9 years

Princess Harimau sighed deeply. She stared through the bars

of the palace windows. She looked out over the pink and white

marble walls of the palace, past the pretty gardens that led

down to the sea. She didn't see the pink flamingoes standing

like statues around the pools. She didn't see the goldfish

swimming under the waterlilies. She didn't see the red and

blue parrots talking in their cages.

Princess Harimau gazed at another group of cages.

These cages contained the king's collection of wild animals.

Many of these animals had been gifts from other countries.

In one of the cages was a tiger called Shiva. Her father, the

king, had given her the tiger on her birthday. Shiva had the

biggest ears, the brightest eyes, and the most enormous paws

Princess Harimau had ever seen.

Shiva sat under the table while the little princess ate her

breakfast. He ran around and around the furniture.

M = Meaning = Does it make sense?
S = Structure = Does it sound right?
V = Visual = Does it look right?

Analysis

E	SC	E M S V	SC M S

Write MSV in the appropriate
column and circle the type
of cue the child has used.

Running Record Sheet

Name: Age: Date:

Analysis

E	SC	E M S V	SC M S

He followed her up and down all the palace stairs. Sometimes

he purred so loudly that she couldn't hear her radio. His tongue

was so rough that she could feel it through her thickest dress.

The little princess forgot about her brothers and sisters.

She forgot about her bicycles. She forgot about her ponies.

She only thought about Shiva.

M = Meaning = Does it make sense?
S = Structure = Does it sound right?
V = Visual = Does it look right?

(214 running words)

Write MSV in the appropriate
column and circle the type
of cue the child has used.

Running Record Sheet

Name: Age: Date:

Analysis

Agatha's Brew (Sunshine, Level 9)
8-1/2 to 9-1/2 years

Agatha poured a bottle of tabasco sauce, two tablespoons

of cayenne pepper, and half a cup of curry powder into the

blender.

"That should make even a jellyfish breathe fire," she said.

Next, she added a cup of salt, a quarter of a bottle of castor oil,

the juice of three green lemons, and a cake of soap.

"And that," she said, "should be enough to make any jellyfish

spit!"

Lastly, she added a whole bottle of vitamin juice (because it

wasn't worth making a magic brew unless it was a strong and

energetic one).

Agatha switched on the blender and watched the sharp blades

whip the mixture into a frothy, yellowy, reddish-brown porridge.

She put her nose over the bowl and sniffed long and deep.

"Wow!" she shrieked.

E	SC	E M S V	SC M S

M = Meaning = Does it make sense?
S = Structure = Does it sound right?
V = Visual = Does it look right?

Write MSV in the appropriate
column and circle the type
of cue the child has used.

Running Record Sheet

Name: Age: Date:

E	SC	E M S V	SC M S

The hairs on the back of her neck stood up like hedgehog

prickles, her ears burned, and her toes curled up in her shoes.

"Wow!" she exclaimed. "That's a powerful potion! I'll call it

Bazooka Brew."

A fly from the ceiling buzzed down and landed on the blender.

It poked its long nose down into the brew and sucked it hungrily.

Agatha watched.

Suddenly the happy buzzing of the fly changed into a roar like

that of a mini-jet at take-off. The fly leaped into the air and

zoomed toward the kitchen window.

"Stop!" cried Agatha. But it was too late.

"CRACK!" The fly hit the window at top speed, and a small,

round, bullet-like hole appeared in the glass.

"Very strong fly!" said Agatha, watching the fly disappear at

supersonic speed. "I might have something here. I better make

sure no nasty bees or spiders or bats get any brew."

M = Meaning = Does it make sense?
S = Structure = Does it sound right?
V = Visual = Does it look right?

Write MSV in the appropriate column and circle the type of cue the child has used.

(283 running words)

Running Record Sheet

Name: Age: Date:

Analysis

E	SC	E M S V	SC M S

Mr. Rumfitt (Sunshine, Level 9)
8-1/2 to 9-1/2 years

Once there was a neat man called Mr. Rumfitt who worked as an

accountant. All the figures he looked at in his office added up to

something, and Mr. Rumfitt thought the world should add up too.

But it didn't.

"It seems to me the world is very badly run," Mr. Rumfitt grumbled.

As he went backwards and forwards in brown buses to and from

work, he thought deeply about this. He decided that what was

wrong with the world was the seasons.

"They are a messy way of arranging things," said Mr. Rumfitt.

"The world should make up its mind what it wants and stick to it.

Just as it gets hot in summer the whole thing turns around and

starts getting colder until wintertime. Then it is cold. Yet is the

world satisfied? No! It starts warming up again — spring,

summer — the whole miserable business gets underway

again, around and around like a giddy roundabout. Mess,

muddle-muddle and mess!"

M = Meaning = Does it make sense?
S = Structure = Does it sound right?
V = Visual = Does it look right?

Write MSV in the appropriate
column and circle the type
of cue the child has used.

90

Running Record Sheet

Name: Age: Date:

Analysis

E	SC	E M S V	SC M S

Mr. Rumfitt thumped with his umbrella every time he thought

about this.

One day Mr. Rumfitt got tired of it all. He took his money from

the bank and bought a valley, out on its own, with a house in it.

He waited carefully until the seasons were between winter and

spring. The trees were bare; the grass was short and tidy.

The weather wasn't very hot and not very cold.

"Neat, very neat!" murmured Mr. Rumfitt, rubbing his hands in dry

satisfaction. He went into his valley and built a wall around it, and

hung a notice on the gate saying, "No seasons allowed."

"That will fix them," muttered Mr. Rumfitt.

M = Meaning = Does it make sense?
S = Structure = Does it sound right?
V = Visual = Does it look right?

Write MSV in the appropriate
column and circle the type
of cue the child has used.

(275 running words)

Running Record Sheet

Name: Age: Date:

The Best Diver in the World (Sunshine, Level 10)
9 to 10 years

E	SC	E M S V	SC M S

Mark walked backward into the water until it reached his waist.

Several times he ducked beneath the surface, allowing the

water to creep inside his wetsuit. Soon his warm body

temperature would heat that layer of water and it would help

to prevent the cold from affecting him so quickly. He tightened his

weight-belt, blew a spray of water out of his snorkel, and wiped

the face of his mask. Turning, he propelled himself gently out

into the bay.

Below Mark was a world of activity. A timid snapper poked its

nose out from under the reef, flicked its tail, and, in a sliver of

flashing silver, was gone. A moray eel, opening and closing its

jaws, backed slowly into its hole. Schools of little reef fish

hustled about their business. A stingray tossed itself and rose

in a cloud of sand. Like a giant butterfly, it glided out of sight.

Then, in the deepest part of the bay, Mark saw the biggest

crayfish he'd ever seen. He backpedaled to a submerged

rock, disarmed his spear gun, laid it on a ledge, and put on

M = Meaning = Does it make sense?
S = Structure = Does it sound right?
V = Visual = Does it look right?

Write MSV in the appropriate
column and circle the type
of cue the child has used.

Running Record Sheet

Name: Age: Date:

Analysis

E	SC	E M S V	SC M S

his thick gloves.

"He's seen something," said a child, watching Mark from the

shore.

"No," replied a more knowledgeable fellow. "He's just getting

himself comfortable."

M = Meaning = Does it make sense?
S = Structure = Does it sound right?
V = Visual = Does it look right?

Write MSV in the appropriate
column and circle the type
of cue the child has used.

(211 running words)

Running Record Sheet

Name: Age: Date:

Tai Taylor Goes to School (Sunshine, Level 10)
9 to 10 years

E	SC	E M S V	SC M S

Have I ever mentioned Tai Taylor and the remarkable tricks he

got up to? Why, when he was a little baby he ... What's that? I

have told you about what he got up to when he was a little

baby, have I? Did I tell you about how he got on when he went

to school? I'll tell you all. Being a hero, Tai needed a special

school and a special teacher. He went to school in a cave and his

teacher was a sort of magician called the Mocker who knew just

about everything, and a bit of magic as well.

Now you might not like the idea of going to school in a cave.

It was full of bats, and bears were always coming in, looking for

somewhere to hibernate. But Tai Taylor was a hero … so he

took no notice of the bats, and he threw the bears out (but

quite gently) and he tried to learn everything the Mocker had

to teach him.

This is what the Mocker taught him at school: reading and

writing to begin with, and mathematics and science (he was

M = Meaning = Does it make sense?
S = Structure = Does it sound right?
V = Visual = Does it look right?

Write MSV in the appropriate
column and circle the type
of cue the child has used.

Running Record Sheet

Name: Age: Date:

E	SC	E M S V	SC M S

doing magnets) to end up with. And in between he learned

useful things like chimney sweeping, how to tune violins (and

the engines of cars), laying bricks, gardening (he was growing

beans and sweet corn), underwater fishing, hang gliding,

pruning roses, embroidery, drainlaying and how to make

chocolate cake.

And he learned artistic things like painting sunsets, and making

new sorts of ice cream, and modern dance, and playing the

electric guitar, and writing poetry about football and cricket.

And he learned all sorts of sports — things like tennis and

hockey and football, and squash. It was a good all around

education.

M = Meaning = Does it make sense?
S = Structure = Does it sound right?
V = Visual = Does it look right?

Write MSV in the appropriate
column and circle the type
of cue the child has used.

(291 running words)

Running Record Sheet

Name: Age: Date:

**The Haunting of Miss Cardamon (Sunshine, Level 11)
9-1/2 to 10-1/2 years**

Sunlight fell like bars of pirate gold where Miss Cardamon

walked, but Miss Cardamon did not see it. A spider's web

wagged in the wind as Miss Cardamon walked by, but Miss

Cardamon wouldn't wag back. Coming out through a narrow

crack in the pavement, grass held up green fingers, but Miss

Cardamon wouldn't shake hands with it.

She was a woman in a hurry. Her step was firm, her eyes were

stern, her back was stiff and straight. She walked in straight

lines whenever she could, and the weedy, wandering ways of

the world were unknown to her. Even the city sparrows stood at

attention when Miss Cardamon walked by.

Miss Cardamon worked at planning the city. She sat in front

of her computer and fed it programs she had written. The

computer fed the city building computers with her instructions

and built the city the Cardamon way. She was good at four lane

motorways, and highrise buildings made of concrete and mirror

glass, but for some reason she was not very good at parks

M = Meaning = Does it make sense?
S = Structure = Does it sound right?
V = Visual = Does it look right?

Analysis

E	SC	E M S V	SC M S

Write MSV in the appropriate
column and circle the type
of cue the child has used.

Running Record Sheet

Name: Age: Date:

E	SC	E M S V	SC M S

or adventure playgrounds.

One day, walking down a perfectly straight footpath, Miss

Cardamon found she was walking behind a very strange,

shaggy woman who looked as if she had bark instead of skin.

As for her dress, it was all ragged at the bottom, with lots of

bright threads hanging down.

"That's a very unfortunate woman," thought Miss Cardamon.

"You can tell she doesn't know how to walk in straight lines."

As she walked, this shaggy woman jingled and jangled because

she was wearing a lot of bracelets and very long earrings. She

was carrying an armful of colored parcels.

As Miss Cardamon watched, the woman dropped her parcels

which scattered in every direction, just as if they were setting out

in the world to seek their fortunes.

"Oh," cried the woman. "My parcels! Could you just help me?"

"I'm sorry," said Miss Cardamon. "I'd like to help you but I only

walk in straight lines and your parcels have gone in every

direction."

M = Meaning = Does it make sense?
S = Structure = Does it sound right?
V = Visual = Does it look right?

(341 running words)

Write MSV in the appropriate
column and circle the type
of cue the child has used.

Running Record Sheet

Name: Age: Date:

The Stranger from the Sea (Sunshine, Level 11)
9-1/2 to 10-1/2 years

E	SC	E M S V	SC M S

Analysis

On the south coast of the island, Thomas lived alone. He loved

to breathe the fresh salt air and to hear the gentle rhythm of the

waves lapping the shore or breaking on the rocks.

Sometimes he thought he would like to share his life with a

wife, a wife who would want to live in his cottage, smelling

the salt air and listening to the waves. But then Thomas would

sigh and put the matter out of his mind.

Night after night, Thomas sat alone in his cottage, listening to

the waves. One night the seas raged, the wind howled, and the

rain beat down. Suddenly, above the sound of the waves

crashing on the rocks, Thomas heard a knock at the door. On

the doorstep stood a man, wet and bedraggled.

"Come and help!" cried the man.

"There's a fishing boat wrecked on the rocks along the coast.

We'll need warm blankets and hot drinks."

Thomas made a fresh brew of tea and poured it into a thermos

M = Meaning = Does it make sense?
S = Structure = Does it sound right?
V = Visual = Does it look right?

Write MSV in the appropriate
column and circle the type
of cue the child has used.

98

Running Record Sheet

Name: Age: Date:

Analysis

E	SC	E M S V	SC M S

bottle. He packed some food into a bag, put on his hooded oilskin

coat, picked up a few blankets and his lantern, then ran down the

path to the beach.

For hours, Thomas worked alongside the other men to help the

crew of the sinking boat. He waded out to the rocks to assist

survivors ashore. One of the men carried to shore a figure so

cold and fragile it was having difficulty breathing. Thomas put

some warm tea into a mug and offered it to the frail form.

Slowly he realized that this was not one of the fishermen from

the wreck, but a young woman.

Thomas turned to the man who had helped her ashore.

"Let us take her up to my cottage. She needs to be away from

this foul weather."

M = Meaning = Does it make sense?
S = Structure = Does it sound right?
V = Visual = Does it look right?

(304 running words)

Write MSV in the appropriate
column and circle the type
of cue the child has used.

Name: Age: Date:

Analysis

E	SC	E M S V	SC M S

Animals at Work (Sunshine, Level 11)
9-1/2 to 10-1/2 years

Animals have made it possible for people to do many things. By

their work on farms, they have helped us to grow many different

kinds of food. They have carted the food to the factories so that

it can be processed and packaged. They have made it possible

for the food to reach people who needed it.

People have used animals to help build houses, roads, bridges,

and even cities. They have made a whole range of industries

possible or easier to run.

Without animals, people would not have been able to communicate

with each other so quickly. They would also have been unable to

travel great distances.

People rode on horses, camels, elephants, and donkeys.

Reindeer, dogs, and horses pulled sleds and carriages and

coaches. Oxen and elephants used their strength to lift or move

great weights. Dogs and horses help people with farm work.

M = Meaning = Does it make sense?
S = Structure = Does it sound right?
V = Visual = Does it look right?

Write MSV in the appropriate
column and circle the type
of cue the child has used.

READING

Name: Age: Date:

Analysis

E	SC	E M S V	SC M S

Today, many of these tasks are done by machinery of some sort.

Animals are no longer needed as much as they once were.

Nor are they needed for the same things. In some parts of the

world, however, animals are as important as they ever were.

They still do the heavy work.

One thing that animals do for people is provide friendship.

Animals that keep us company, comfort the sick, guide the blind,

and keep us safe will probably always be needed.

M = Meaning = Does it make sense?
S = Structure = Does it sound right?
V = Visual = Does it look right?

Write MSV in the appropriate
column and circle the type
of cue the child has used.

(212 Running words)

Notes

Notes

Notes